Outside of Time

Outside of Time

Poems by

Carol Mikoda

© 2025 Carol Mikoda. All rights reserved.
This material may not be reproduced in any form, published,
reprinted, recorded, performed, broadcast,
rewritten or redistributed without
the explicit permission of Carol Mikoda.
All such actions are strictly prohibited by law.

Cover design by Shay Culligan
Cover image by William Justen de Vasconcellos on Unsplash
Author photo by Curtis Corlew

ISBN: 978-1-63980-806-9

Kelsay Books
502 South 1040 East, A-119
American Fork, Utah 84003
Kelsaybooks.com

for Steve

Acknowledgments

Thank you to the following publication, in which this poem previously appeared:

Capsule Stories: "Outside of Time"

Contents

I.

While I Look the Other Way	15
How Lost We Really Are	16
Message	17
Misnomer	18
Missed Again	19
Crossing	20
Preparation	22
In My Midnight Kitchen	23
Lighting Up the Brain	24
Counting Game	27
new perspective	29
Questioning Vonnegut	30
Time Travelers	31
The Fox Who Is Also There	34
When the Time Comes	35

II.

Spirit vs. Clock	39
Not a Day Earlier	40
dog days slinking in	42
When the Snow Geese Rise	44
Without Narrative Arc	45
Outside of Time	46
Dancing Through Time	47
Seeker	48
as I chop onions	50
Then We Were Dancing	51
Half-Life Sonnet	52

Waiting	53
Daily Destruction	54
Stay	56
Today Is the Day	58
Music That Leaks Across Light Years	60
Lost and Found	62
Just in Time	63

*Time flows in the same way for all human beings;
every human being flows through time
in a different way.*

~Yasunari Kawabata

I.

We don't understand the first thing about time.

~Kurt Vonnegut

While I Look the Other Way

A haze of green
spreads on the forest floor
as leaves build up strength
and bulk to pop out of twigs.
The most ordinary thicket
of thorn bushes
takes on a magical patina
as though washed again
and again with pale color,
coat after coat,
all afternoon. In tomorrow's
sunlight, I will not
remember how slowly it gathers
before it explodes.

How Lost We Really Are

Times are urgent; let us slow down.
~a saying of the Yoruba people of West Africa

The wild wind rages in the treetops; gulls
bob on the water, trying to be one with the white caps.
Swells, filled with the contagious energy of existence,
gallop past. Swallows surge in their intricate
loops. Tall grasses lining the roads
bow their heads in perfect time with the wind,
making their own rules of rhythm and harmony.

How lost we really are, we who spend
our time pushing and pulling, putting and placing,
if we do not hear the streams dance or witness
the earth's art in stone, in sycamores, in sunflowers.

Message

Today the green leaves
speak. They
         whisper,
     "We lack nothing.
The world belongs to us:
          this day,
        this moment." They
           tremble
with their message,
            flame
into orange,
     red,
      yellow,
        wilt,
      then   fall
    into murmuring piles.

Misnomer

What you call time
drips from me
as if sprayed from a hose
I keep trying to discard,
leaky thing
dappled with mildew,
misshapen by frosts,
bulbous here,
kinked up there.

I try to name each drop
as a certain day or hour
but it slips away unpinned.
I wonder, "Monday?
Or Saturday?"
I can't remember
pills, words, names,
all sorts of things
I think I want to remember,
yet unbidden memories
flood each day.

I could coil them up
and trash them
like the old hose
but some of them bring
showers of love,
nourishment for anemones,
something to move
when the music comes by.

Missed Again

This is when the ginkgo dropped its leaves
in a gold blanket of carbon, nitrogen, spent chloroplasts
that lit the grass with the energy of an entire summer.

This is when the ginkgo dropped its leaves:
before dawn as first frost crystals formed;
after other trees let go of their last in heavy rains;
on a morning so quiet that the sound of air
passing through the flying crow's wings
floated above the newly yellow field.

This is when the ginkgo dropped its leaves:
after all the others had been pushed back
into a crispy barricade at woods' edge;
as the geese flew south one morning
under the fading face of the full moon about to set;
when the devil, dressed as a woman, set off fireworks
and knocked on doors asking for candy.

This is when the ginkgo dropped its leaves:
just before the white dust of first snow fell at dusk;
in the sudden calm before the wind changed;
when I had looked the other way.

Crossing

On this journey,
nothing is explained;
everything is possible.
I keep walking
though I sometimes
wish for an
end to it.
I continue to take
step after step,
day by uncertain day.
I stop to rest
for a breath or two,
to feel the wind,
to look ahead
or glance back,
where the past recedes
faster and faster
though I seem
to continue at
the same pace.
As always, I
hear restless water.
As I round
a turn, I see
last week's ice
piled like old blankets
carelessly thrown
on the rocky shoreline,

I hear it asking,
"What awaits me?"
Ever the question.
Never an answer
except to be here,
now, poised
to go forward.

Preparation

The owls call and call at dusk
in a language you do not speak.
The fullness of the wind
presses against you.
You look out at the dark waters,
across whitecaps
that leap and jostle,
always moving,
infinity of choreographed dolphins
that seem to warn
of cataclysm looming,
approaching from the top of the lake.
You feel you must get ready.
But somehow their breaching
and dancing reassure you:
this is not the end.

In My Midnight Kitchen

I'm making bone broth.
The suffering of past years
browns in olive oil;
I scrape the good bits
from the bottom of the pot
as the three sisters join:
carrot, onion, and celery.
Bay leaf and thyme sprigs
swim in the simmering chalice
through the pre-dawn dark.
As the sun rises,
I fill a bowl with acceptance
of whatever is present now,
and also
now.

Lighting Up the Brain

I. The Past

\<shivers\>

regret seems to reign but
after all is said and done

\<cold wind glides through,
shadow passes over\>

gratitude overpowers
regret with warmth
and the power
of daily practice

II. The Future

<surrounded by darkness>

What tea is best served
with Fear and Uncertainty?
I find Earl Gray a bit perfumy
for my tastes now,
but Hibiscus is good
for blood pressure?

<debilitating lack of control>

I have made my decision:
I believe the universe
is friendly,
and is working
in perfect harmony
with me?

<peering through the fog>

III. The Present

Accept circumstances.
Greet feelings and then
let go. Breathe. Repeat.

Counting Game

Standing on the porch
I can hear the waterfall.

But I turn my attention
to the sunlight's play
on sumac's laddered leaves.

I count each small leaf
on one side, then the other,
spoken numbers sitting
calmly on my tongue,
lining up for the next,
like cards in a game of solitaire,
like the ceaseless dripping
of time and tears, like the rain
of years that surprise me
from month to month speeding
as they do past every milestone
or benchmark until I want
to give up, not mark time in any way,
throw the whole lot of them
into the fermenting stewpot
marked PAST and be left alone
with a simple counting game:

one downward fluttering
yellow leaf, another, and another,
until they fill the air
and cover the ground at my feet.

My balance is threatened
by these gales that gallop
toward autumn and winter,
but I stand firm inside
the gold blizzard.

new perspective

atop graveyard hill,
a reminder: life is here,
now, in earth's beauty.

sit in a cemetery
        looking at life
lie back
        in the browning grass
        of summer
peer at the clouds
stare long at stars' silence
or into moon's blue vacancy
let the wind rustle
        in your branches
breathe in the sultry passion
        of soil and smoke
open your throat
        to earth's banquet
open your arms
accept the gift of freedom

Questioning Vonnegut

Not the most satisfying conversation, but I had no expectations, really. It was, as expected, an insufferably humid afternoon in the Mohawk River valley. We sat across from each other at one of the high tables just outside the rusty gates of a dingy bar in downtown Schenectady, he with his Scotch and water, me with my vodka and tonic. After all my years of reading his morbidly comical work, I had so many questions. Could you tell me what you think about Truman? About FDR? "In time, in time," he answered. Do you look forward to a reunification of South and North Korea under a single puppet government controlled by another Asian state? "In time, in time," he intoned, puffing on his latest cigarette. Will I know God? "In time." He gave no other answer. Even when I asked him to write me a letter, he only said, "In time, in time," sipped on his Scotch, and smiled amiably at me. That meeting happened in another world, at another time, and I am still waiting.

Time Travelers

I.

We drape ourselves in the soft
winding cloth left behind
in the tomb after a resurrection.
Its quantum powers allow us to slide
along the gentle curves
of the space-time continuum,
until we settle into a century, decade,
year, season, where we feel
most seen, least afraid.
We leave a culture that values us little
to go to one where we feel cherished,
purposeful, one where we belong.

II.

You may look out
at these vistas we gaze on
and see misty mountains,
disintegrating stone walls,
expanses of silky lake water.
Where we are, ancient ruins
might be newly constructed,
or might have fallen away,
taken back into the soil.
Mountains may be leveled,
lakes dried up, replaced
by plowed fields or a city.
Time reveals all as malleable.

III

I see by your expression
that you are intrigued, confused:
We return, in this way,
in order to spread the word
to those who search among pills
and chemicals for release.
We have found that release
another way, in another place,
another time.

The Fox Who Is Also There

I am there
when the wind changes.
From the dock,
I watch choppy water
that has no aim or sure direction.
It is quiet when the air,
no longer meandering from the south,
veers to drive from the west,
coming at me across the lake.
The cottonwood leaves grow loud,
branches lift behind me,
as I watch the water skid and sway,
trying to catch up with energy's shift.
When I turn to leave,
I see the fox,
the fox who is also there
when the wind changes,
the fox,
a rusty streak
leaping across my path
up through the hill's thick brush.

When the Time Comes

"When the time comes," she
tells them, "unplug me.
It appears I can't
do that myself, connected
as I am with this
delivery system,
clicking and tapping
with the oxygen
and water of our
time, the digital
wonder of unseen
charges and jots and tittles,
pulses that cannot be sensed . . ."
(sipping some water)
". . . at our wrists. Darkness
will fall upon me,
not unwanted, nor
entirely dark." Spent,
she turns back to her device.

II.

Only time, whatever that may be, will tell.

~Stephen Hawking

Spirit vs. Clock

The many clocks
ticking on the mantel
in the living room
set my blood
to pulsing with them.
I breathed in minutes,
digested hours,
my sweat sticky
with seconds.

Deep inside,
my holy heart
struggled to reach
field and forest.
I collapsed on the moss,
taking slow deep breaths,
free at last
from the trickster tyranny
of time.

Not a Day Earlier

Walking each day
I open my heart
as the hawk announces
its hunting plans overhead

the windy lake throws down
its sound as a carpet
for my thoughts and steps

the large stone I pass
draws my gaze when
water and light gild it just so

mist above cold water
in the warm sunlight—
did I see it once before?

my heart says no—
never just that way
nor clouds that rip and tear
apart, sailing overhead
nor felt the heat rippling
off the road
until this time

I must read this world
as different every day
as a unique message
from a universe that knows well
[who I am today
and never was before]

knows what time it is
in my heart—time
to cherish the gilded stone
discern the hawk's true message
read the clouds as never before
not a day earlier
not an hour later.

dog days slinking in

the dog star that's risen is mad
or at least doesn't know its own mind
chaos in the shed
from raccoons' night fury
air hums from incessant insects
the fizz of summer
replaced by the fever
of a single mosquito
whining in the ear as
sky bears down; ground presses up
grass dies from boredom
prays for broken mowers
I walk along the lake
with my feet in the water before dawn
watching for drafts
that make leaves flop and twist
wading geese do not move
when I approach nor make a sound
pockets of cooler air surprise
then disappear just as fast
stagnant pools try to evaporate
from the creek's rocks and crannies
but it almost takes too much effort
indoors, rodents die and disintegrate
cats too sleepy to chase them
odors accumulate despite fans
whirring in every room
just drape me over a lawn chair
in the shade of the trees

let the sprinkler,
the one keeping the carrots alive,
wave its wet arms at me once in a while
as I wait for breezes to resume
for fevers to break
everything changes
comes to some end
turns to something else
a net of clouds at sunset
gathers pink, gold, and peach
pallid days become
chill nights filled with stars
we watch from our blankets on the lawn
as they take us to infinity

When the Snow Geese Rise

When the snow geese rise

in parallel lines

from marsh and stubble's texture

into gray flannel clouds,

their flight paths

crosshatch the slant

of falling snow. It's time,

they cry, insistent

rising notes matching altitude.

Corn carries them south

as fields release

the last of their riches.

Without Narrative Arc

Crescent moon
follows set sun
to earth's edge.

Well worth
day's wait
for such charm.

We rest.

Another day comes
when earth twirls
its precise ballet
across a dark stage
dusty with stars.

We play on that stage,
in that black cold,
too dark to read cue cards.

There are none.

We ad lib
our own garbled scripts,
block out our own
lurching action.

Unlike the earth,
we get one show.

It lasts a lifetime.

Outside of Time

As if you could kill time without injuring infinity.
~Henry David Thoreau

He thought that was a joke
but here we are killing time, bludgeoning it,
and still it stretches out before us like a carpet
that needs vacuuming, tattered curtains hanging
on either side limiting our vision, cobwebs
stretching down to our faces from god knows what
above us. We have no choice but to keep
walking, step by step, along this corridor
we ourselves constructed, somewhere way back
in intellect's unfolding. We look anxiously ahead.

If only we could sit a spell, let the eternal carpet
roll on without us for a bit. This is hard work,
sometimes paralyzing, and not so productive. Maybe
we can meditate, detach ourselves from this pointless path
and see something more perfectly open, more loving and true,
hidden behind the ripped curtains, where trees
and small animals whisper of our whereabouts
and watch us from a world outside of time.

Dancing Through Time

Years roll by like lake water through a broken
dam; I am the broken dam, and the lake water
rolling through the break. I'm the fish swimming
to new waters. I'm the galleon cloud looming
over lake and leaves. I'm wind moving cloud ships
over field and forest. I am heat rising from far
oceans to create storms that swirl around
our peopled sphere. I also dance, a dervish
in a trance; I step with surety and abandon. I loose
the lengths of silk that wrap me. All but essence
swings away. Protons, neutrons guide
movement, step airily from ionization.
Patterns push the agenda stars have had
since before they exploded away from oneness. We dance
back toward that oneness with integration written
into our atoms, undeniable, under
the surface of everything we do. We exert our will
but still the pull of this prescription makes itself
known. Every lick of life strives
back toward that sheltered place of unity, back
where it all began, where it never ends, where nobody
expects dams to break or folds of silk
to slowly slide away.

Seeker

When a bell finds your ear at midnight, and the death cry
of a small animal wakes you, rise up. Take only
what is important: your voice, your imagination, your heart,

even if it is a long way from the truth. You can coax it closer.
Start walking. Stop at every crossroads to ask many
questions about a star's death and the traps

of what you already know.
Listen for vibrations set off by shapeshifters. Keep walking,
reaching to the light. Reach to the edges. Keep soaring,

though altitude is not the point.
As you travel, tend your heart's fire. In this life-long
conversation between loss and joy, surprises come;

wisdom follows. Use your freedom to free others;
acknowledge the jewels you meet among the ashes.
Bring them with you to sit at the rough-hewn table

in that clearing at the heart of things, where every seat fills
and the great mad poets of yesteryear drop in just to listen.
When the trees of every color let loose their birds

and throw down their shadows, then dance with fireflies
and mountains, sing with snails and mushrooms. Dream.
Weep. Grieve beneath the stars, and notice how grief

shrinks with every breath, how light gets through.
As your body collapses, you become more lucid. Suffering
disappears like a white heron flying into morning mist.

as I chop onions

as I chop onions, celery,
      sauté them
to make dressing for the feast
young men try   to entertain me
their inventions distract me for a bit
return to
      the pan and the oil and the sizzle
the sharp tears
    forget them
in their haze and cry of look-at-me

don't be frightened
      none of this is real
even as you drift between decades
all things will be well
too bad we can't see the big picture
return to the chopping the oil the sizzle

for it is all that matters

Then We Were Dancing

Then we were dancing
as if decades had not
passed, families had not bloomed
and faded, children all grown,
parents, marriages, here and
gone, a slow explosion
of time until only we two were left
and the world misted over,
disappeared from our
circle of steps where we leaned in
and listened only to the music,
our breathing, and the muscles
we moved together.

Half-Life Sonnet

Perhaps the dark cries we hear today
are from yesterday's
stars. What's it like, to be alone,
lost, in space and time, blazing away?
We don't know how it feels,
all that energy, constant
burning that intensifies, building, surging, always
barely out of control over eons until expansion
reaches its end. Wouldn't we cry out
in fear of the yielding
to dusk that is inevitable?

I am crying out now.
Tomorrow my children will hear.

Waiting

Sometimes waiting is all we can do.
So we lie here in the dark and listen:
Water falls against stone. High winds
thrum through cables. Or maybe rain
slaps down on the metal roof. Crickets
measure the night, one degree at a time.
A metallic crash, broken glass, bedsheets
slide. Pencils scratch paper, paper crumples,
leaves rustle in a corner tornado.

Sounds fade as thoughts again intrude, shivering
in the anxious gusts of awareness like poplar
leaves turning and turning, whispering,
muttering answers. Then we cross
the border into the bardo and see
everything, glistening and silent.

Daily Destruction

Walking is falling forward . . . an act of faith.
~Paul Salopek

On a daily basis,
I lift my feet,
one at a time,
to pitch forward
again and again,
tumbling my way
down the hill
into the lake's moods,
into the arms
of nature
that walks with me.

My heart also breaks
anew each day:
lone chicory blossom
stranded on the roadside,
sunlight slanting in
to gild an afternoon,
the stare of a hovering
hummingbird,
an owl's call
flooding the darkness
of a sleepless night.
With each wound
I am opened
a little more,

making room
for more beauty,
for seeds of compassion
to lever in more deeply.

Stay

after Galway Kinnell

Don't go yet.
The lake view opens up now,
through branches losing their foliage,
emptier by the minute.
Stay and count the yellow leaves
following their wild spiral paths
from tree tops.

It's difficult, this world.
But stay to hear whatever it is the wind says
while it echoes oceans.
Feel the sun on your shoulder
through soft flannel and tattered clouds.
Interpret the pattern of leaves on green lawn,
at every angle, organically shuffling
with change in mood
and countercurrent.

Today, hear the wind,
try to follow the swirling blizzards
of summer's late kingdom,
bask in warm rays.
Tomorrow brings other obsessions
along with pain, trouble, cold,
and the rest of that.

But to miss this bluster and confetti,
this sunlight and shadow,
would wound in another way.
So to you I say,
stay.

Today Is the Day

when everything changes:
Sand rises from its bed
near the water, lifted by gusts
strong enough to draw
it into a wet tornado.

Every tree shows its soul,
every fish, every flower,
and those four flamingos, too,
flying through the dawn
to find shrimp.

Summoned from business
as usual into a field
of action and love,
I follow the faint path
that veers to the left.
Gifts from strangers
in wayside cottages
help me on my way.

A glass mountain looms;
I fight my way up through spider
webs of steel, but I delight
in the music their filaments
vibrate with the wind.

I call out to my wild twin,
the one lost at birth, who
sits, meditating, at the top.

Music That Leaks Across Light Years

Listen: lean toward that tiny flicker of wings,
the pale silence of joy flitting
from one human flower
to another on its way to you.
It travels like light,
faster than your eyes
even if they are open to amazement
as well as the troubles of the world.
You might detect the whoosh,
the delicate vibration
of a rainbow of color frequencies,
or a hummingbird's resting breaths.

Breathe with it—enter its sphere
and take on its perspective
from that branch in the fir tree.
Survey the universe made small,
then leap from the branch,
arc through the rain
toward the western sun and beyond.
Jump to a new perch.

Stand tall on a mountain's peak,
so close to the stars that their music leaks
across light years to move
your feet and arms,
in a dance that connects you
with the ancestor gods who came before.

They dance within you as a reminder
to seize joy whenever it dips down
to bless your head bowed with sorrow and stress.
It brings you its lightness, speed, and motion.
It is tucked inside the patches of blue sky
between clouds of all seasons.

It follows after the swoop of a hawk toward its survival,
after the slide of a newborn from its mother's womb,
after the skid of your feet against gravel
when your balance is challenged.
Rise up with joy and find your way.

Lost and Found

We are lost every day, whether we know it or not.
Holy water trickles over the stones of our lives
from an unknown source and makes its way
to an unknown hollow, bearing us along,
with or against our wills. We do not alter
our heading with our feeble strokes and kicks.
Why not swim with that power?

So we turn over to float on our backs,
looking up at the stars, soaring birds,
tossing tree limbs. We watch the wind
combing the clouds with its unseen currents;
we catch the sunny sparkles of wavelets it generates.
As we drift, we see white birds that drape
the oaks and cypress like discarded underwear,
amid strands of Spanish moss. Formations
of pelicans shepherd their children over the waves
next to us. Flocks of smaller birds pass over us.
Whales and dolphins find us as they dance.

Just in Time

I wake up from late August stupor
to a fall breeze, cool and soothing,
a calm hand to summer's fevered
forehead. A line of sound, raindrops
on the lake at the storm's leading edge,
tells me that I will not reach you
before it arrives and washes away
the fragile sidewalk chalk art
the two of us have created together,
but I will be there in time to feed
the cats and make dinner with you.

About the Author

After a long career as an educator, Carol Mikoda now spends much of her time writing poetry. Under the influence of ee cummings, Rumi, Hafiz, Bashō, Millay, Oliver, and others, she writes poems filled with nature and spirit, from her yellow table above Seneca Lake in central New York State.

Her work has appeared in many literary journals, most recently *Wild Greens, Inkfish,* and *Blue Heron Review*. Her first chapbook, *While You Wait,* is available from the author; her second, *Wind and Water, Leaf and Lake,* is available from Finishing Line Press. Her prose poem, "Jesus at the Pub," was nominated for Best of the Net and The Pushcart Prize. She has strong attachments to clouds, trees, water, and music. Contact her at caro.miko@gmail.com or through The Yellow Table on Substack.

www.ingramcontent.com/pod-product-compliance
Lightning Source LLC
Chambersburg PA
CBHW031205160426
43193CB00008B/507